NEW YORK

Portrait of a City

NEW YORK

Portrait of a City

GRAPHIC ARTS™ BOOKS

Second Printing
Library of Congress Control Number: 2006926480
International Standard Book Number: 978-1-55868-987-9

Captions and book compilation © 2006 by
Graphic Arts™ Books, an imprint of
Graphic Arts Center Publishing Company
P.O. Box 10306, Portland, Oregon 97296-0306
503/226-2402; www.gacpc.com
The five-dot logo is a registered trademark of
Graphic Arts Center Publishing Company.

President: Charles M. Hopkins
Associate Publisher: Douglas A. Pfeiffer
Editorial Staff: Timothy W. Frew, Kathy Howard, Jean Bond-Slaughter
Production: Susan Dupèré
Cover Design: Vicki Knapton; Interior Design and Captions: Jean Andrews

Printed in the United States of America

Front cover / Title Page: ● The Brooklyn Bridge, among the oldest suspension bridges in the country, reaches 5,989 feet across the East River to connect Brooklyn and Manhattan.
Back cover: ● Central Park's Strawberry Fields, a 2.5-acre memorial to John Lennon, features an inlaid stone mosaic, which is often decorated with flowers in honor of the slain songwriter and musician.
◄◄ Although the New York State Legislature received a petition for a bridge between Brooklyn and Manhattan in 1802, it took until 1883 before the Brooklyn Bridge was finally opened.
◄ European settlement of the area now known as New York City began with the founding of the Dutch fur-trading settlement of New Amsterdam in Lower Manhattan in 1613.
► The Queensboro Bridge connects the neighborhood of Long Island City, Queens, with Manhattan, passing over Roosevelt Island.

◄ Restaurants, bank services, retail
stores, and more occupy space in the 102-story
Art Deco–style Empire State Building, finished in 1931.
▲ Urban skyscrapers really do seem to "scrape" the sky.

▲ LEFT TO RIGHT: Everywhere one looks, Greenwich
Village presents a plethora of detailed design. Examples are:
● A stairway, obviously created for more than functionality; and
● A building's exterior embellished with intricate carvings.
▶ Spring green in Greenwich Village sets off a
row of brownstone apartments.

◄ The Flushing 1964–65 World's Fair *Unisphere*
rests in the Flushing Meadows–Corona Park, Queens.
▲ The Verrazano-Narrows Bridge is a double-decked
suspension bridge that connects Staten Island and Brooklyn.
►► South Street Seaport harks back to the nation's swashbuckling
maritime heritage: tall sailing ships and a thriving seaport.

Pier 16
CIRCLE LINE
HARBOR CRUISES
Pier 16
CIRCLE LINE
HARBOR CRUISES
NO SMOKING

▲ The Plaza is situated on 5th Avenue, across
from the southeast corner of Central Park in Manhattan.
The French chateau–style hotel opened to the public in
1907, and was awarded landmark status in 1969.

▲ The Fountain of Abundance is in the
Grand Army Plaza adjacent to the hotel known to
New Yorkers as simply "the Plaza." Newspaper publisher
Joseph Pulitzer's will stipulated $50,000 to be used to create the
fountain. The statue in the fountain is Pomona,
the Roman goddess of abundance.

▲ The United Nations Headquarters is
accented by its member nations' colorful flags. The
eighteen-acre site on Manhattan's east side is an international
zone belonging to all member states. The complex has served as the
United Nations headquarters since it was completed in 1952.

▲ First established in 1904, the Jewish Museum
has been a major cultural institution. With more than
28,000 objects, the museum offers one of the most extensive
collections of its kind in the Western Hemisphere.

▲ Clockwise from top left:
Wildlife, both in zoos and outside them, thrives in New York City.
● A snowy egret, *Egretta thula,* wingspan 38 inches, takes flight on Long Island;
● A red panda, *Ailurus fulgens,* looks out at the world from Central Park Zoo; and
● A Cuban alligator, *Crocodylus rhombifer,* waits for prey at the Bronx Zoo.
► A magnolia tree, also called a "saucer" magnolia, brightens Central Park.
►► The New York Philharmonic performs in Central Park.

◄ Holiday decorations at Rockefeller Center are always
a highlight of the season for New Yorkers and visitors alike.
The Christmas tree, 75 to 100 feet tall, is only the centerpiece.
Angels, lights, and picturesque ice skaters add to the ambience.
▲ The outdoor Wollman Rink in Central Park South is a
popular place for skaters to be in cold weather.

▲ St. Marks Place in East Village got its name from the
original St. Mark's Church in-the-Bowery, built in 1660 by Peter
Stuyvesant to serve as the family's private chapel. The present church was
consecrated in 1799 as an Episcopal church and continues to serve in that capacity.
▶ Between 1892 and 1954 some twelve million immigrants came through Ellis Island and the
Port of New York. The Main Building, now the Ellis Island Immigration Museum, and the
American Immigration Wall of Honor attract visitors seeking a piece of their history.

◄ A hotdog vendor sells his wares at
42nd Street and Madison Avenue in Midtown Manhattan.
▲ The Plaza's atrium restaurant, the Palm Court, is famous for its afternoon tea.
►► Times Square is the happening place for New Yorkers and visitors
alike. Restaurants, hotels, stores, Broadway theaters, music, and
colorful advertisements are only a few of the attractions.

◄ Crown Tower, with arguably the most
interesting roof in the area, sits in the shadow of Trump World
Tower, but the larger tower doesn't detract from the beauty of the Crown.
▲ *The Phantom of the Opera*, at the Majestic Theater, is the longest-running
show in Broadway history. The New York production alone has played
to more than ten million people in its nearly twenty-year run.

▲ Numerous decorations embellish
New York buildings. Here, copper adds a delicate
patina to the window frames of a building.

▲ High-rise residential towers have long been the choice of developers in Manhattan's West Side. Living high above the city is part of a lifestyle enjoyed by many New Yorkers.

▲ Vesuvio Bakery has been a fixture on Prince Street since
1920. It is known in Soho for its picturesque bread displays.
► Trump World Tower rises above Manhattan and the East River and is
one of the world's most luxurious residential towers, with homes
that sell for up to thirteen and a half million dollars.

◄ Radio City Music Hall opened to the public in 1932. Situated
in Rockefeller Center, it is known as the Showplace of the Nation.
▲ Apollo Theater, Harlem's top attraction, does much to reach out into the
community with such programs as Free Films for Kids. Many famous people,
including Ella Fitzgerald, James Brown, Michael Jackson, D'Angelo, and
Lauryn Hill, have launched their careers at the Apollo.

▲ The American International Building, in Manhattan, was built from 1930 to 1932.

▶ The Conference House, a colonial manor home in Tottenville, Staten Island, was the site in 1776 of a peace conference between the colonists—represented by Benjamin Franklin, John Adams, and Edward Rutledge—and the British—represented by British Admiral Lord Howe.

▶▶ Washington Square Park, in the heart of Greenwich Village, is characterized by its large, central fountain and triumphal stone arch.

◄ Traditionally, the buildings lining Park Avenue
have been the most expensive and sought-after in town.
▲ John F. Kennedy International Airport has been operated
by the Port Authority of New York and New Jersey since 1947. The
airport takes up some five thousand acres of what used to be marshlands,
a golf course, and more. Originally named New York International,
its name was officially changed in December 1963.

▲ A mural depicting the *Statue of Liberty* decorates a wall.

▶ The Flatiron Building got its name from its shape (like a flatiron).
It was said that the building created unusual eddies in the wind
that would cause women's skirts to fly around as they walked
on 23rd Street. This attracted throngs of young men
who gathered to view the bare-legged spectacle.

◄ Flowers add a delicate touch to a shop in Soho.
▲ Grand Central Station now incorporates restaurants,
cocktail lounges, international eateries, gourmet foods, and
specialty shops—all in addition to transportation.

▲ *Lunchtime on a Skyscraper—*
A Tribute to America's Heroes in Long Island City,
Queens, was created by Sicilian artist Sergio Furnari.
His work is characterized by sculptural "slice of life"
figures, rather than important political figures.

▲ The *Sherman Monument,* a sculpture
of Civil War general William Tecumseh Sherman,
is made of bronze with a gold leaf surface. A woman
representing victory strides in front of the horse. The palm
branch in her left hand represents peace. New York sculptor
Augustus Saint-Gaudens completed the statue in 1903.

▲ LEFT TO RIGHT: Each year Macy's, the famous
department store in Herald Square, decorates for Christmas:
● Evergreens with Christmas lights create a "forest" above the entrance; and
● A Christmas tree created entirely with lights nearly covers the clock
above the entrance. A forest of a different kind lines the street
as small trees carry the decorations down the sidewalk.

▲ The newly hip, picturesque Bedford Street is situated
in the Williamsburg area on Brooklyn's north side. History is alive and
well here, including: a house built in 1799; a farmhouse built in 1807; and the city's
narrowest building—three stories tall and just ten feet wide—built in 1873.

▶▶ An aerial view of Midtown Manhattan, the busiest commercial
district in the nation, shows the offices, hotels, and retail stores
where more than three million commuters work.

▲ The New York City skyline
presents a golden view of the Big Apple.
▶ The Manhattan Bridge, Midtown, and the 1,250-
foot-tall Empire State Building seem to form layers
that rise ever higher with each structure.

◄ A game of chess in Bryant Park
attracts both participants and observers.
▲ Even golf practice New York City–style
is a multistoried activity.

▲ "Bombs bursting in air" silhouette the
Empire State Building in a Fourth of July celebration.
Macy's traditionally sets off fireworks in several areas around
the city, and the U.S. Air Force does a patriotic
flyover before the fireworks begin.

▲ Tiny, twelve-acre Liberty Island,
situated in New York Harbor, is home to one
of America's greatest icons—the Statue of Liberty.
►► Created by sculptor Emma Stebbins, the *Bethesda Angel* was
placed in Bethesda Terrace of Central Park in 1873.

◄ CLOCKWISE FROM TOP LEFT:
Central Park provides scenery and activities year-round—
⦁ Walking paths, carpeted with fall leaves, winding among the trees;
⦁ Ball fields dotting the Great Lawn, inviting players and spectators;
⦁ Autumn bringing colorful leaves along with joggers; and
⦁ Old-time carriage rides, available year-round to visitors.
▲ Boating is also a favorite activity in Central Park.

▲ Since 1914, Gertel's Bakery has been a landmark on
New York's Lower East Side. Gertel's offers more than three
hundred bakery items every day, besides breakfast and lunch choices.
▶ Pretzels New York–style are available from many sources—
street vendors, restaurants, and bakeries—but they
are always best served fresh and warm.

◀ Saint Patrick's Cathedral is an example of the style of Gothic
church architecture common in Europe in the thirteenth century.

▲ LEFT TO RIGHT: New York City tends to be vertical. Examples are—

● The *Peace Fountain* beside St. John the Divine Cathedral in Harlem; and

● Trinity Church with its tall steeple dwarfed by office buildings on Wall Street.
New York's oldest church, Trinity was chartered in 1697 by King William III,
but it burned in 1776. The present church was dedicated in 1846.

▲ William H. Seward, secretary of state
from 1861 to 1869, is probably best known for
negotiating with Russia for the purchase of Alaska—referred
to at the time as "Seward's Icebox" and "Seward's Folly."
The statue, located in Madison Square Park, was the
first to be erected in honor of a New Yorker.

▲ The Gold Key Russian Deli is situated
in Brighton Beach, Brooklyn, an area known
as Little Russia. Brighton Beach has become home
to a large Russian émigré population.

▲ The Blue Note Jazz Club, located in the heart of Greenwich
Village, is just one of the city's numerous entertainment venues.
▶ A Rock 'n' Roll Artist Mural adorns the Blue Note Jazz Club.
▶▶ The highly photographed Brooklyn Bridge forms
a colorful backdrop to the South Street Seaport.

◄ At the American Museum of Natural History, four
floors of exhibits cover numerous scientific findings, including
the foot of a *Barosaurus*. The name *Barosaurus* means "Heavy Lizard,"
which refers to its 66- to 88-foot length and its weight of approximately 44 tons.
▲ The trip to Long Island can be as much fun as getting there; the
ferries incorporate comfort with an enjoyable boat ride.

▲ The New York Stock Exchange exhibits a patriotic face.
The Stock Exchange began in 1792 when twenty-four stockbrokers
signed the Buttonwood Agreement under a buttonwood tree. Nicknamed the
"Big Board," the New York Stock Exchange is the world's largest in dollar volume.
▶ A pizza restaurant on the Lower East Side has its own way of expressing
patriotism—with a flag-and-eagle mural painted on its door.

◀ At night, a lake in Central Park holds
the reflections of lights from nearby buildings.
▲ The Triborough Bridge is not just one span; it actually
encompasses three main bridges, plus smaller bridges
and viaducts. It also includes fourteen miles of
approach highways and parkways.

▲ The many faces of Times Square
include shops, retaurants, hotels, entertainment,
and images of celebrities.

▲ A massive planter bursting with
colorful flowers is an early sign of spring
on the Mall of Central Park.

▲ The 7,000-pound bronze *Stock Market Bull* statue, also called the *Charging Bull* or the *Wall Street Bull,* was created by Arturo Di Modica in 1989 and placed in front of the New York Stock Exchange—illegally. Public opinion in its favor was so strong, however, that officials decided not to destroy it. Instead, they moved it to Bowling Green Park, where it remains today.

▲ Isamu Noguchi's *Cube*, erected in 1967, stands
at the corner of the Marine Midland Bank building in lower
Manhattan. Building designer Gordon Bunshaft originally proposed
a monolith-like sculpture, but it was deemed too expensive.

▲ The George Washington Bridge, designed by
Othmar H. Ammann, is a suspension bridge across the
Hudson River. The original six-lane bridge was opened to traffic in
1931. In 1946, two more lanes were added. Some thirty-five years after the
original bridge's construction, Ammann served as consultant for the
design and construction of the lower level of the bridge, which
increased the capacity of the bridge by 75 percent.

▲ The Metropolitan Museum of Art, located on
5th Avenue in Manhattan, is one of the world's largest
art museums. Often referred to simply as The Met, it houses
approximately two million works of art from around the world.
▶ TOP TO BOTTOM: Murals present a kind of folk art—
◗ A Black theme adds color and interest to a wall; and
◗ Real shoppers join virtual ones in front of a store.

◄ The clock above Tiffany's 5th Avenue entrance is held up by a
figure of Atlas. The clock has adorned the entrance since 1853 when it was
created by Henry Frederick Metzler, a friend of the store's founder, Charles Tiffany.
▲ Citigroup Center was built to accommodate St. Peter's Lutheran Church, which
occupied one corner of the site. The fifty-nine-story tower is set on
columns at the center of each side, so the building soars seventy-
two feet over the church nestled under one corner.

▲ Sculpted by Edward Clark Potter, two lions guard the entrance of the
Main Branch Public Library. Although the lions have been given various names
through the years, New Yorkers simply refer to them as "Uptown" and "Downtown."
▶ Lincoln Center for the Performing Arts is actually a complex of buildings encompassing some
sixteen acres. It was the first U.S. complex to gather multiple cultural venues in one place.
▶▶ The Hayden Planetarium, able to create sophisticated shows of the solar system,
is the largest and most powerful virtual reality simulator in the world.

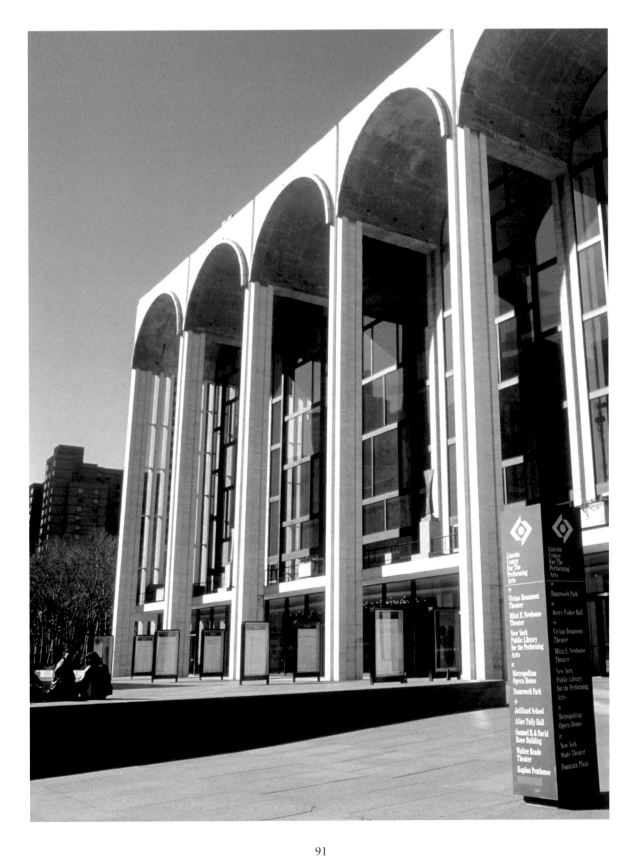

◄ World-renowned for more than a century, the Waldorf=Astoria
started as two hotels: one built by William Waldorf Astor in 1893 on
the present-day site of the Empire State Building, and the other owned by
his cousin, John Jacob Astor IV, called the Astoria Hotel. Today's Art Deco
building combines the two hotels; hence the name Waldorf=Astoria.
▲ Thousands of wooden water tanks dot the city, making it possible
for buildings taller than six stories to have water pressure.

▲ The first ferry between Brooklyn and Manhattan
was a rowboat operated by Cornelius Dircksen in 1642.
Today, 145,000 vehicles per day cross the Brooklyn Bridge.
The bridge, including approaches, spans 6,016 feet.

▲ The *Prometheus* statue, situated at Rockefeller
Center, is one of the most famous sculptures in America,
second only to the Statue of Liberty. Prometheus was an Immortal
who stole fire from Zeus and gave it to the primitive mortals
on the earth. John D. Rockefeller commissioned sculptor
Paul Manship to create the statue in 1933.

▲ TOP TO BOTTOM:

Sights in Manhattan's Chinatown include—

● Signs in Chinese, mixed with a cacophony of languages; and

● Brightly colored Chinese lanterns decorating the front of a shop.

► A golden Chinese lion embellishes a Chinese-red entrance.

►► The Solomon R. Guggenheim Museum, designed by
Frank Lloyd Wright, was established in 1939.

◄ Bloomingdale's, on 3rd Avenue, has
been offering its premier shopping experience since 1927.
▲ The ceiling of the Jacob K. Javits Convention Center gives a glimpse
of the size and intricacy of the structure. Built in 1986, it was designed by
architect I. M. Pei and was named for New York Senator Jacob K. Javits.
The exhibit space encompasses more than 675,000 square feet.

103

▲ The Lower Manhattan skyline rises beyond the
Brooklyn Bridge, as seen from the nearby Manhattan Bridge.
▶ The Burnett Fountain accents the English Garden, one of three
formal gardens in Central Park's six-acre Conservatory Garden.
The child holding the birdbath is Mary, from Frances
Hodgson Burnett's book *The Secret Garden*.

◄ Soho showcases the exterior fire
escapes so prevalent throughout New York City.
▲ Cobble Hill, a Brooklyn neighborhood, was part of the
"Brownstone Revolution," a movement designed to restore the area's
brownstone and brick row houses, built in the mid-nineteenth century.
►► Historic Richmond Town is a living history village and museum
complex covering twenty-five acres on Staten Island.

▲ A sidewalk cafe in Soho gives
an intimate look at a relaxed lifestyle that
counters the stereotype that New York is all rush-rush-rush.
▶ Natural beauty in New York City is found in its parks and zoos,
but beauty of another kind is inherent in the buildings themselves.
▶▶ Built in 1963, the skyscraper originally called the Pan Am
Building was bought in 1981 by MetLife for $400 million.